I0448760

Comptroller of the Currency
Administrator of National Banks

Floor Plan Loans

Comptroller's Handbook
(Section 210)

Narrative - March 1990, Procedures - May 1998

A

Assets

Floor Plan Loans
(Section 210)

Table of Contents

Floor Plan Loans
(Section 210)   Introduction

Floor plan, or wholesale, lending is a form of retail goods inventory financing in which each loan advance is made against a specific piece of collateral. As each piece of collateral is sold by the dealer, the loan advance against that piece of collateral is repaid. Items commonly subject to floor plan debt are automobiles, large home appliances, furniture, television and stereo equipment, boats, mobile homes, and other types of merchandise usually sold under a sales finance contract.

This type of financing involves all the basic risks inherent in any form of inventory financing. However, because of the banker's inability to exercise full control over the floored items, the exposure to loss is generally greater than in other similar types of financing. Most dealers have minimal capital bases relative to debt. As a result, close and frequent review of the dealer's financial information is necessary. In analyzing that data, it is important to review the number of units sold and the profitability of those sales. A comparison should be made between the number of units sold and the number financed to ensure that inventory levels are not excessive. As with all inventory financing, collateral value is of prime importance. Control over that requires the bank to determine the collateral value at the time the loan is placed on the books, to continuously inspect the collateral to determine its condition, and to impose a curtailment requirement sufficient to keep collateral values in line with loan balances.

Two important facets of the bank's relationship with a dealer are the quality of the paper generated and the deposit account maintained. The income derived from a floor plan loan may not be sufficient to justify the credit risk. A bank often looks to the additional income derived from good quality loans to purchasers of the dealer's inventory. If the bank is not receiving an adequate portion of loans generated by the dealer or if the paper is of inferior quality, the relationship is of questionable value to the bank. The deposit account represents both a compensating balance and a tool by which the loan officer can monitor customer activity. A review of the flow of funds into and out of the account may reveal that inventory has been sold without debt reduction, that the dealer is incurring abnormal expenses, or that unreported diversification, expansion, or other financial activity has occurred that might warrant a reconsideration of the credit arrangement. Token or overdrawn balances should trigger increased collateral inspections.

In most banks, the evidence of debt is the trust receipt. There generally are two methods by which trust receipts are created. The bank may enter into a drafting agreement, similar to a letter of credit, with the manufacturer. In this situation, the bank agrees to pay documentary drafts covering shipments of merchandise to the dealer. The drafts are payable at the time the merchandise is received or, if the manufacturer permits, after a grace period which allows the dealer to prepare the inventory for sale. The drafting agreement usually provides a clause for cancellation and limits the number of units, the per unit cost, and the aggregate cost that can be shipped at one time. These restrictions tend to prevent a manufacturer from forcing excessive inventory on a dealer They also permit the bank to cancel or suspend shipments of unwanted merchandise. Drafting agreements frequently are made in conjunction with repurchase agreements under which the manufacturer agrees to repurchase merchandise that remains unsold after a specified period of time. The merchandise and related title documents remain with the dealer until sold and are evidenced by a trust receipt. All the documents should be inspected physically during the floor plan inspection to prevent dual financing.

Trust receipts also are created when merchandise is shipped under an invoice system. The dealer receives the merchandise accompanied by invoices and titles, where appropriate. The dealer presents the documents to the bank and the bank pays the invoice, attaching duplicates of the documents to a trust receipt that is signed by the borrower. Depending on the type of inventory and/or the dealer, the title may remain in the bank or be released. Used car inventories usually are financed under trust receipts with a listing of the units and their loan values attached to the receipts. The method of perfecting a security interest varies from state to state, and there are numerous divergencies from the Uniform Commercial Code. The examiner should determine that the security interest has been properly perfected.

With title documents and collateral in the possession of the borrowing dealer, the bank must have an established procedure for flooring verification. Flooring check sheets should be on file in the bank, indicating that a bank representative has personally verified every article, by serial number and description, shown by bank records as unsold and in the dealer's possession. The condition of the floored articles must indicate that they are available for sale. Any missing articles or other exceptions revealed by the flooring check, as well as the dealer's explanation thereof, must be verified as proper. Missing items reportedly sold and unpaid must be verified to related contracts in process, and such processing time must be reasonable. Floored items sold and not in process of payment represent breach of trust by the dealer, and the amounts owed represent unsecured credit.

An inherent weakness in any floor plan loan is the banker's inability to exercise full control over the collateral. The examiner must determine whether the banker is verifying the collateral, that is, the inventory being financed, on a frequent basis. The scope of inspections must be sufficiently broad to detect irregular activity. Inspection duties should be rotated among the department's staff, and the floor planned inventory should be verified by the audit department during the regularly conducted audits.

A serious warning signal is evident when inventory has been sold and the bank's loan has not been repaid. If inventory is missing at the time of each floor plan inspection and the dealer then remits, it is a sign that the dealer may be taking advantage of a float, i.e., using proceeds of inventory possibly sold weeks before the inspection rather than remitting promptly as required. There are very few examples of dealers selling inventory "out of trust" which are permitted by bankers. Dealers selling in large volume are usually granted a three-day leeway before proceeds from inventory sold are required to be received by the bank. This permissible time lag allows the dealer to conduct the amount of necessary bookkeeping at his place of business. If it is disclosed that a dealer is deliberately withholding funds received from the sale of pledged inventory collateral, the bank should terminate the customer relationship immediately.

Because loan advances are made on 100 percent of the collateral value, as the collateral begins to depreciate, the individual loan amounts should be curtailed. The collateral may depreciate if used as a demonstrator, is no longer a current-year model, or was previously owned (used) when floor planned.

A typical dealer of any product must maintain a reasonable inventory. It will generally be the dealer's principal asset, and its acquisition will normally create the dealer's major liability. The dealer's financial statement must show an inventory figure at least equal to the related flooring liability as of the date of the financial statement. Unless the difference is represented by sales receivables, including contracts in transit, a flooring liability that is greater than the amount of inventory is an indication that the dealer has "sold out of trust."

A dealer who, by diverting the funds received, has sold portions of his merchandise "out of trust" leaves the bank with a portion of its flooring line on an unsecured basis.

Situations where the bank only finances a portion of the dealer's floor plan debt originating from a particular manufacturer or distributor should be avoided. Bankers are able to exercise only minimum control over financed inventory under the best arrangement. Delinquent notes, either unpaid interest or lack of required curtailments, and maturities extended beyond reasonable expectation are warning signs. These signs indicate that the dealer is hard pressed for liquid working capital and should alert the banker to conduct collateral verification inspections more frequently. Slow moving inventory, other than farm equipment or other seasonal merchandise, could be a sign of poor management on the part of the dealer.

The credit review of floor plan loans usually is assigned to the examiner who appraises indirect dealer lines in the installment loan department. Before the credits are transferred to the examiner performing the review of credit files, the floor plan examiner should have performed all procedures related to the existence of the related collateral and its value. The bank's policies and procedures should be clearly defined with compliance noted. Controls over the borrower must be in evidence. Collateral values should be supported by source documents or bank appraisals. Any deficiencies within the department must be discussed with management by the examiner in charge of "Floor Plan Loans" before the review of credit files is undertaken.

General Procedures

Objective: Develop a preliminary assessment about the quantity and direction of risk and the quality of risk management for floor plan lending. This assessment will be used to determine the scope for the floor plan lending examination.

Review the following documents to identify any previously identified problems related to the floor plan lending area that require follow-up:

- ☐ Previous examination reports.
- ☐ Management's responses to previous examination findings and other bank correspondence.
- ☐ Ongoing supervisory comments.
- ☐ Working papers from previous examinations.
- ☐ Internal loan review reports.
- ☐ Internal and external audit reports.

(Note: If an examiner is assigned "Internal and External Audit," a copy of any significant deficiencies for this area should be obtained from that examiner. If Internal and External Audit is not part of the overall scope of the examination, review the work performed by the internal and external auditors in this area and obtain a list of any deficiencies noted in their most recent review.)

Review the Uniform Bank Performance Report (UBPR), BERT, and the bank's current risk assessment to identify trends within the portfolio.

Obtain and analyze reports management uses to supervise floor plan lending:

- ☐ Schedule of curtailment requirements for each dealer.
- • Schedule of approved floor plan lines for each dealer including outstanding balances.
- ☐ Delinquent curtailment billing report.
- ☐ Drafting agreements and amount of outstanding drafts.
- ☐ Delinquent interest billings, date billed, and amount of past due

interest.
- ☐ Risk rating reports.

The analysis should consider:

- Growth and acquisitions.
- New product and services for floor plan lending.
- Management changes.
- Policy and underwriting changes.
- Changes in risk limits.
- Changes in such external factors as:
  - National, regional and local economy.
  - Competition.

Obtain from the examiner assigned "Loan Portfolio Management" the following schedules, if applicable to this area:

- Past due loans.
- ☐ Exception reports.
- ☐ Participations purchased and sold since the preceding examination.
- ☐ Loans sold in full since the preceding examination.
- ☐ Loan commitments and other contingent liabilities.
- ☐ Extensions of credit to major shareholders, employees, officers, directors, and/or their interests.
- ☐ Extensions of credit to officers and directors of other banks.
- ☐ Miscellaneous loan debit and credit suspense accounts.
- ☐ Loans considered "problem loans" by management, denoting those loans added by officer/management since the last examination.
- ☐ Loans classified during the preceding examination.
- ☐ Information on directors, executive officers, principal shareholders, and their interests.
- ☐ Each officer's current lending authority.
- ☐ Current interest rate structure.
- ☐ Any useful information obtained from the review of the minutes of the loan and discount committee or any similar committee.
- ☐ Reports furnished to the loan and discount committee or any similar committee.
- ☐ Reports furnished to the board of directors.
- ☐ A listing of rebooked charged-off loans.

Determine, during early discussion with management:

- How management supervises floor plan lending.
- Any significant changes in policies, practices, personnel, and control systems.
- Any internal or external factors that could affect floor plan lending.
- Management's perception of the credit culture for floor plan lending.

Based on the findings and analyses of the previous steps and in consultation with the EIC and other appropriate supervisors, determine the scope of this examination.

Select from among the following examination procedures those steps that are necessary to meet examination objectives. Examiners should tailor the procedures to the risks identified in their findings and analyses discussed with the EIC.
Note: Examiners will seldom be required to complete every step.

As the examination procedures are performed, test for compliance with all applicable laws, rules, and regulations and with established policies. Confirm the existence of appropriate internal controls. Identify any areas that have inadequate supervision or pose undue risk, and discuss with the EIC the need to perform additional procedures or testing.

Quantity of Risk

Conclusion: The quantity of risk is (low, moderate, high).

Objective: To determine the quantity of risk in the floor plan lending portfolio by evaluating the adequacy of collateral, credit quality, and collectability and assessing compliance with applicable laws, rulings, and regulations.

1. Obtain a trial balance of all floor plan accounts and:

    - Agree balances to department controls and general ledger.
    - Review reconciling items for reasonableness.

2. Review the information received from management and the Loan Portfolio Management examiner.

3. Select loans, using an appropriate sampling technique, which require in-depth review based on information derived from the review above. Transcribe the following information, for each borrower selected, onto the credit line sheets:

    - Total outstanding liability.
    - Number of items.
    - Status of any outstanding interest or curtailment billings.
    - Amount of approved floor plan line.
    - Information from the bank's collateral record, including:
        - A list of items floored, including date of entry, description of property, amount advanced, and curtailment, if any. (Similar items and model year should be shown in aggregate and entry dates shown as a range, except on stale or not properly curtailed items.)
        - A brief of the wholesale agreement between the bank and the dealer.
        - A brief of the agreement between the manufacturer and the bank.
        - A brief of any repurchase agreement.
        - Evidence that security interest has been perfected.
        - Details of any guarantees that may be held.
        - Details of any other collateral held.

---

4. Review the two most recent floor plan inspection reports, and:

- Determine the reason for differences between the bank's collateral records and the actual items held by the dealer.
- Trace those items represented as sold or in process at the time of inspection to their subsequent removal from the bank's liability ledger.
- Determine the number of days between the sale date and removal from liability ledger.
- Using the above information, review the dealer's deposit account(s) and determine whether the dealer may be withholding funds received from the sale of the pledged collateral.
- Investigate other differences to the extent considered necessary.
- Determine if any items were sold out of trust.
- Determine that where trust receipts are used, all title documents were physically inspected during the floor plan inspection.
- Determine whether appropriate follow-up was made on all missing items.

5. If floor plan inspection procedures are considered deficient or if they are not performed on a timely basis, perform physical inspection of collateral on sample basis.

6. Review participations purchased and sold.

- Test participation certificates and records, and determine that the parties share in the risks and contractual payments on a pro rata basis.
- Determine that the books and records properly reflect the bank's liability.
- Investigate any participations sold immediately prior to the examination to determine whether any were sold to avoid possible criticism during this examination.

7. Review extensions of credit to officers and directors of other banks. Investigate any circumstances that indicate preferential treatment.

8. Review miscellaneous loan debit and credit suspense accounts.

- Discuss with management any large or old items.
- Perform additional procedures as deemed appropriate.

9. Review loans classified during the previous examination, determine disposition of loans so classified by transcribing:

   - Current balances and payment status, or
   - Date loan was repaid and sources of payment.

10. For loan commitments and other contingent liabilities, analyze if:

    - The borrower has been advised of the contingent liability.
    - The combined amounts of the current loan balance and the commitment or contingent liability exceeds the cutoff.

11. Review rebooked charged-off loans and determine that the rebooked loans:

    - Meet the criteria and terms of the bank's lending policy for granting new loans.
    - Are not subject to classification. If so, list the loans for charge-off.

12. Based on the findings from the preceding activities, determine, in consultation with the LPM examiner, whether the following verification procedures should be completed. If so, using appropriate sampling technique, select floor plan loans, and:

    - Prepare and mail confirmation forms to dealers (information confirmed should include the loan balance and the schedule and date of items floored).
    - After a reasonable time period, mail second requests.
    - Follow-up on any no-replies or exceptions, and resolve differences.
    - Compare title documents and/or invoices to trust receipts.
    - Obtain a list of the most recent floor plan interest billings, and check calculation of interest report.
    - Determine whether interest payments are delinquent, and trace to inclusion in delinquency report.
    - Determine that appropriate action has been taken to bring delinquent

accounts to a current status.

- Test trial balance reconciling items to the extent considered necessary.

Quality of Risk Management

Conclusion: The quality of risk management is (strong, satisfactory, weak).

Policy

Conclusion: The board (has/has not) established effective policies regarding floor plan lending.

Objective: To determine if floor plan lending policies are adequate.

1. Determine whether the board of directors, consistent with its duties and responsibilities, has adopted written floor plan lending policies that:

    - Establish procedures for reviewing floor plan applications?
    - Define qualified borrowers?
    - Establish minimum standards for documentation?
    - Establish curtailment guidelines, including providing proper incentives to the dealer to turn over inventory on a timely basis?

Processes

Conclusion: Management and the board (have/have not) established effective processes regarding floor plan lending.

Objective: Determine the adequacy of risk management processes regarding floor plan lending.

1. Determine whether floor plan lending policies are reviewed at least annually to determine if they are compatible with changing market conditions.

2. Determine the adequacy of floor plan loan administration practices.

    Floor Plan Agreements
    - Are floor plan agreements required for all dealers?
    - Must agreements be accompanied by borrowing resolutions?

- Is a written agreement between the manufacturer and the bank required on any flooring line that includes drafting arrangements with the manufacturer?
- Do such agreements with the manufacturer stipulate under what conditions the bank will accept items to be floored?

Financial Information
- Are dealers required to submit financial and operating statements on a continuing basis?
- Are all dealers who prepare internal financial and operating statements more frequently than annually required to submit copies of those statements to the bank?
- Are all financial statements received from dealers reviewed promptly?
- Do financial statement reviews include a determination that floor plan loans, deposit accounts, and other information agrees to the bank's records?

Floor Plan Line Limits
- Are all floor plan loans granted under an established line?
- Are line approvals structured to permit the bank to cancel or suspend shipments of unwanted merchandise?
- Are dealer floor plan line limits strictly adhered to?

Disbursement of Funds
- Are disbursements for floor plan loans on new units made only against the original copy of the manufacturer's invoices?
- Are the original invoices retained in the bank's files?
- Are loan proceeds on new units paid directly to the manufacturer rather than to the dealer?
- Are accounting records established so that the bank has records of all floored items with adequate individual identification?
- Are limits on loan advance versus invoice price (current wholesale value, if used) clearly established?
- Are wholesale values determined independently of dealer appraisals?
- Are wholesale values that are assigned by floor plan department personnel periodically reviewed by someone independent of the department?
- Is amount of loan advance prohibited from exceeding 100 percent of the invoice price of a new item or of the wholesale value of a used

item?

Payments
- Are floor plan interest charges systematically computed and regularly billed?
- Are notices of past-due interest payments sent promptly?
- Are all interest, curtailment, and unit pay-off payments from dealers posted promptly?

Curtailment
- Is the loan written so that the floored items never depreciate faster than the loan balance is reduced?
- If the manufacturers of the floored items have entered into a repurchase agreement, are curtailments structured to keep the loan balance in line with any declining repurchase amount?
- Are records maintained on curtailment billings so that delinquency is easily determinable?
- Are notices of past-due curtailment payments sent promptly?
- If assignment of rebates has been made, have procedures been established to insure that factory rebate checks payable at the end of the model year are promptly forwarded to the bank?
- If demonstrators are floored, are they subject to separate curtailment requirements that keep the loan balance in line with their liquidating value?

Miscellaneous
- Is a trial balance of each dealer's trust receipts/security agreements prepared at least monthly?
- Are dealer trial balances reconciled to department and general ledger controls?
- Are periodic reviews made of deposit accounts, to detect any possible out of trust sales?
- Are periodic reviews made of the retail paper being generated to determine if the bank is receiving an adequate portion?

3. Assess the adequacy of the collateral administration practices.

Inspections

- Are floor plan checks, physical inventories, conducted at least monthly and on a random surprise basis?
- Are more frequent floor plan checks required if the dealer is experiencing financial difficulties?
- Are individuals performing floor plan checks rotated?
- Are floor plan inspector(s) required to determine or verify the following and indicate their findings on the floor plan check sheet:
    - Serial number of item?
    - Odometer reading of vehicles?
    - Condition of item?
    - Location of item, if other than normal place of business?
    - Existence of any fire or theft hazards?
- Does the floor plan inspector include on the check sheet:
    - Date inspection was performed?
    - Date any item located elsewhere was checked?
    - His or her signature?
    - Summary of his or her report, if appropriate?
- Are all demonstrators checked?
- Are floor plan reports reviewed by an officer?
- Are follow-up inspections made of items not seen during the regular inspection?
- Are items reported by the dealer as being sold, required to be paid off immediately?
- Does the floor plan inspector determine the date that item(s) reported as sold were sold from that on the dealer's copy of the sales agreement?
- Are dealer sales patterns reviewed to determine that the number of units reported sold at the time of floor plan inspection is not excessive and does not indicate a float?
- Are payments in process reported by the dealer during floor plan inspection verified by bank personnel?

Trust Receipts
- When a dealer trade or "swap" occurs, does the bank:
    - Obtain the manufacturer's invoice from the selling dealer on the new unit acquired?
    - Obtain the invoice from the borrowing dealer for the new unit?
    - Have a trust receipt executed on the new unit?
- Does the bank have a procedure to check all indirect paper received

from a dealer against the trust receipts of items floored for that dealer to determine that there is no duplication of loans against the same security?

- Are all trust receipts required to be supported by invoices or other evidence that title to the security is vested in the bank?
- Are trust receipts required to include:
  - Description of each item?
  - Serial number of each item?
  - Loan amount for each item?
  - Interest rate?
  - Date?
  - Authorized signature of dealer or person holding power-of-attorney to execute the trust receipt?
- If the bank and dealer permit a bank employee to execute trust receipts using the dealer's power-of-attorney:
  - Are proper documents on file granting the power-of-attorney?
  - Does the bank maintain a numbered register for trust receipt notes?
  - Are trust receipt notes under dual control?
  - Are checks made periodically to determine that only those individuals granted power-of-attorney are signing the trust receipts?

Insurance
- Does the bank have floor plan property damage insurance or require that the dealer maintain such coverage with the bank named as loss payee?
- Is the insurance coverage periodically reviewed for adequacy?

4. Assess the adequacy of internal control processes regarding floor plan lending.

Floor Plan Loan Records
- Is the preparation and posting of subsidiary floor plan loan records performed or reviewed by persons who do not also:
  - Issue official checks or drafts singly?
  - Handle cash?
- Are the subsidiary floor plan loan records reconciled daily with the appropriate general ledger accounts, and are reconciling items

investigated by persons who do not also handle cash?

- Are delinquent account collection requests and past-due notices checked to the trial balances used in reconciling floor plan subsidiary records with general ledger accounts, and are they handled only by persons who do not also handle cash?
- Are inquiries about loan balances received and investigated by persons who do not also handle cash?
- Are documents supporting recorded credit adjustments checked or tested subsequently by persons who do not also handle cash (if so, explain briefly)?
- Is a daily record maintained summarizing note transaction details, i.e., loans made, payments received, and interest collected, to support applicable general ledger account entries?
- Are frequent note and liability ledger trial balances prepared and reconciled with controlling accounts by employees who do not process or record loan transactions?
- Is an overdue account report generated frequently (if so, state frequency _____)?

Loan Interest
- Is the preparation and posting of interest records performed or reviewed by persons who do not also:
  - Issue official checks or drafts singly?
  - Handle cash?
- Are any independent interest computations made and compared or adequately tested to initial interest record by persons who do not also:
  - Issue official checks or drafts singly?
  - Handle cash?

Personnel

Conclusion: The board, management, and effected personnel (do/do not) possess the skills and knowledge required to manage and perform duties related to floor plan lending.

Objective: Given the size and complexity of the bank, determine if bank management/personnel possess and display acceptable knowledge and technical skills in managing and performing duties related to floor plan lending.

Determine if the staff size is appropriate given the size, complexity, and level of risk in the floor plan lending portfolio.

1. Assess bank managers/personnel knowledge and technical skills related to floor plan lending based on conclusions developed while performing these procedures.

Controls

Conclusion: Management (has/has not) established effective control systems.

Objective: Determine the effectiveness of control systems employed to manage floor plan lending.

1. Determine the scope and adequacy of the internal and external audit function. Consider:

   - Scope of review.
   - Frequency of reviews.
   - Qualifications of audit personnel.

2. Obtain a listing of audit deficiencies noted in the latest review performed by internal and external auditors from the examiner assigned "Internal and External Audits." Determine if management has appropriately addressed noted deficiencies.

3. Determine the adequacy of the loan review function. Consider:

   - Scope of review.
   - Frequency of reviews.
   - Qualifications of loan review personnel.
   - Results of activities in the Quantity of Risk section of these examination procedures.

4. Obtain the most recent loan review report on floor plan lending. Determine if management has appropriately addressed noted concerns.

5. Determine the adequacy of management information systems (MIS). All

evaluations of MIS should assess timeliness, accuracy, level of detail, clarity of report format, and distribution channels. Consider:

- Past due and nonaccrual status.
- Risk ratings.
- Loan yield and profitability data.
- Trend analysis.
- Commitments, industry type, amount and level of expected usage, and highest usage on record.
- Maturity categories.
- Exceptions to policy, underwriting, and documentation standards.

6. Has the board or senior management established adequate procedures for ensuring compliance with applicable laws, rulings and regulations?

- For compliance with the bank's legal lending limit, the examiner should combine total outstanding floor plan indebtedness with all other indebtedness, including the dealer instalment paper, with recourse, the borrower has sold to the bank.

7. Are internal controls for the floor plan lending department appropriate for the level of risk in the portfolio?

8. Determine the adequacy of any other control systems employed by management to supervise floor plan lending.

Conclusion

Objective: To communicate findings and initiate corrective action when policies, practices, procedures, objectives, or internal controls are deficient or when violations of law, rulings, or regulations have been noted.

1. Provide EIC with brief conclusion regarding:

    *   The adequacy of written policies relating to floor plan loans.
    *   The manner in which bank officers are conforming with established policy.
    *   Schedules that were discovered to be incorrect or incomplete.
    *   The quality of departmental management.
    *   Internal control deficiencies or exceptions.
    *   Other matters of significance.

2. Determine the impact on the aggregate and direction of risk assessments for any applicable risks identified by performing the above procedures. Examiners should refer to guidance provided under the OCC's large and community bank risk assessment programs.

    *   Risk Categories: Compliance, Credit, Foreign Currency Translation, Interest Rate, Liquidity, Price, Reputation, Strategic, Transaction
    *   Risk Conclusions: High, Moderate, or Low
    *   Risk Direction: Increasing, Stable, or Decreasing

3. Determine in consultation with EIC, if the risks identified are significant enough to merit bringing them to the board's attention in the report of examination. If so, prepare items for inclusion under the heading Matters Requiring Board Attention.

    *   MRBA should cover practices that :
        –   Deviate from sound fundamental principles and are likely to result in financial deterioration if not addressed.
        –   Result in substantive noncompliance with laws.
    *   MRBA should discuss:
        –   Causative factors contributing to the problem.
        –   Consequences of inaction.

- Management's commitment for corrective action.
- The time frame and person(s) responsible for corrective action.

4. Discuss findings with management including conclusions regarding applicable risks.

    - Delinquent loans, including breakout of "bad" debts as defined in 12 USC 56.
    - Extensions of credit to employees, officers, directors, and/or their interests.
    - Loans on which collateral documentation is deficient.
    - Recommended corrective action when policies, practices, or procedures are deficient.
    - Other matters regarding the condition of the department.

5. As appropriate, prepare a brief floor plan lending comment for inclusion in the report of examination.

    - Quantity of risk.
    - Quality of risk management.

6. Prepare a memorandum or update the work program with any information that will facilitate future examinations.

7. Transfer liability and other pertinent information to examiner assigned to "Installment Loans." Credit review will be performed in conjunction with the analysis of dealer indirect lines.

8. Update the OCC's electronic information system and any applicable report of examination schedules or tables.

9. Organize and reference working papers in accordance with OCC guidance.